AF434153

DO Y.O.U.

(YOUR OWN UNIQUENESS)

CRYSTAL JACKSON

Crystal Jackson
Do Y.O.U.

All rights reserved
Copyright © 2023 by Crystal Jackson

No part of this publication may be reproduced, distributed, or transmitted in any form or by any means, including photocopying, recording, or other electronic or mechanical methods, without the prior written permission of the publisher, except in the case of brief quotations embodied in critical reviews and certain other noncommercial uses permitted by copyright law.

Front cover photo designed by Chase Mack

Published by BooxAi

ISBN: 978-965-578-092-5

CONTENTS

DEDICATION

*I dedicate this entire book to the Barley and Jackson Clan and all my friends and extended Family. I am inspired and challenged to always keep the J.O.Y. (**Jesus** FIRST Front and Center Stage), **Others** (family and friends) and also remembering to take care of **YOU**) myself.*

To my encourager and fighter until the end, my dad, the late and great Deacon Maple Barley, Jr. Your parent-ship and wise nuggets will NEVER be forgotten. I will forever honor and celebrate you DAD!

Thanks so much to the late Tanya Thompson. Her edits helped me produce this product and pushed me to continue even two months (November 2021) before her transition. I will always cherish your friendship, love and support.

You have to be the best Y.O.U. (Your Own Unique-ness) can be! YOU are the only YOU!

Always

#doyou

FOREWORD

This book was penned to inspire, encourage, and empower ANYONE who is challenged in discovering and defining Y.O.U. (*Y*our *O*wn *U*nique-ness)!

When all the rest falls apart, you only have one thing
to fall back on... and it's YOU!
Because we are fearfully and wonderfully made,
crafted by our Master and Maker of life,
if YOU fall, remember,
He can mend YOU back together again.
YOU have to believe in Y.O.U.! (*Y*our *O*wn *U*nique-ness)!

INTRODUCTION

When our children were younger (ages two and three), after getting them fully dressed, I would stand them in the mirror at home and say, *"Good morning my Prince! Good morning my Princess! You are royalty! We claim <u>NO</u> lack in this home!"* By the age of seven, our son Kary would ask me, *"Mom, who are you?"* I would say, *"I'm the Queen and your dad (Kary, Sr.) is the King!"* Day in and day out, these phrases did not change.

When Kary, our oldest child, entered school, he encountered criticism from teachers and schoolmates, saying his clothes were too expensive and his parents spent too much money on dressing him. He was an honor roll student in the National Honor Society....earning all A's and 1B throughout Middle and High School. Kary received numerous of scholarships for college. During his years in college at Lamar University, he made the Dean's list, served as a Peer Advisor for several years, and continued to maintain high-standing grades until he graduated. Yes, he is a Prince because we treated him as such! However, not only did we dress his outside appearance, we dressed his mind and equipped him to know who he is and how to discover his Y.O.U. (**Y**our **O**wn **U**nique-ness)!

While in High School, Kayla, our other unique child, encountered several people calling her names and misunderstanding her. Kayla developed her own style and made many major fashion statements. She dressed to impress herself. I remember Kayla wearing two different colors of shoes to school. She loved her converse tennis shoes as well as all of her favorite Michael Jordan sneakers. She was really our different *"unique"* child. She too, made the National Honor Society and graduated from Lamar University, majoring in Fashion Design. Even though she was vocal and spoke her mind, she made sure you understood and knew where she was coming from. She had a temper that could accelerate very high and she would confront her peers and teachers. Yet instilled in her was always a little small voice that said to her on numerous occasions, *"I am a Princess! I am Royalty!" I don't stoop down to their level."* Her favorite saying was, *"I'm not a chicken; I soar with eagles."* She continues to live by this mantra, as evidenced by the status of living she currently maintains.

As our children grew older, they were continuously reminded of who they were and who they should become. God had already purposed them to be great!

God has a purpose for all of us. God made each of us in His image, in his likeness; therefore, you are who God says you are. You can be whomever you want to be. You can go whatever you want to go! You are your greatest asset. Y.O.U. can be a *plus* or a *minus*. The decision is definitely yours.

CHAPTER 1
Y.O.U. WERE CREATED ON PURPOSE

"Our presence here on the earth is in preparation for an awesome and amazing future!"

Lady Cj

Mark Twain said, *"There are two great days in a person's life – the day we were born and the day we discover why."*

God created us in "His own image" and likeness (Genesis 1:27). We were fearfully and wonderfully made and born for a purpose! Each of us was created for a reason.

When we were born, we did not have a choice of whom our parents were going to be. We could not walk into a store and say, *"I want my dad to be 6'1, weigh only 210 pounds, and have light skin, brown hair and no freckles."* Nor could we say, *"I want my mom to be 5'6, weigh only 110 pounds (you know we like to be little), have almond color complexion, black hair, flaw-less skin and no pimples."* (Ha!) Truth be told, only God knew who our parents were going to be. Only God knew who we were going to be.

I often wonder, what was God's purpose for creating us (*humans*)? I ponder so many thoughts and questions all the time. Did God create humans because he needed someone to relate? Was he bored and one day, He became creative and produced a universe that included people like you and I? Some speculate that God wanted or needed human relation-ships, so He created us to remove his own aloneness. One big problem with this thinking is that it implies something is lacking in God. God is perfect, nothing can be lacking.

When God created us, he showed genuine love, He placed us in a dominion to live in, gave us authority over creation, and granted us freedom.

God has an incredibly valuable task for us. God has prepared specific works for each of us to walk in. That is called walking into your purpose. We must tap into our purpose to do greater works here on earth. Many people have not discovered their purpose because they do not believe they have anything to offer. God has given each of us gifts to help others and to let our light shine.

God created us to live an amazing life. He created us to live in a way that glorifies Him. When He created this world, He made a statement at the end of each day of His creation. He appraised and applauded His own work. God said, *"It's good!"* At the end of the sixth day, he looked at Adam and Eve and said, "It's very good!" This means that God did not do things with mediocrity. God has amazing capacities. I believe He is truly pleased with what He had done.

Many people have no idea of what life is all about. They live and they die, searching for some kind of meaning, not knowing their lives have a purpose. Do you know where you fit? You really matter in the grand scheme of things.

While growing up during high school, some people were voted *"Most Popular;" "Most Likely to Succeed;"* King and Queen of the Homecoming Court; or even Valedictorian, but all too soon, youthful plans and dreams evaporated into anxiety and frustration because of so many missed opportunities, failed relationships, or countless other *"if-only"* and *"might-have been."* How many times you have said, *"I wished I would have... done this or done that."*

I am so reminded of the story of the wisest man who ever lived, Solomon. He was an ancient king of Israel. He was in search to find the purpose of his life and what he thought was the real source of happiness. He sought to do *everything*. He explored the proverbial wine, women, and yes, many WOMEN. He had 700 wives and 300 concubines (*mistresses*). He built palaces, acquired great wealth and his fame spread all across the world.

Solomon eventually realized that in the end, we all will die and cannot take anything with us. This realization sent him into depression and created so much anxiety that he even contemplated suicide. He said, "all was vanity and a grasping for the wind.... therefore I *hated* life." (Ecclesiastes 2:11, 17-20). Solomon learned that seeking physical experiences and acquiring possessions does not bring real fulfillment. There is such a far greater purpose for life.

Having a purpose gives us life and energy. Many people die empty with unfulfilled lives. Solely seeking gratification from money, sex, power, respect, or popularity means little. We will all die, and none of these things can be taken anywhere with us. Life is so much more than that because God offers each of us so much more. He offers us true significance and purpose. There is so much joy in being what He created us to be.

We are not an accident. Never consider yourself as one. Again, we were designed and wonderfully made on purpose. God gave us lives significance. God created us to live in the freedom, joy, and beauty of His design. However, when we look at our lives and our world, we see that something went wrong. When we look at individuals, families, communities, churches, and this nation, we see news that bring sorrow and heartaches. The news is filled with stories of murder every day, death every day, famine every day, divorce every day, ethnic cleansings every day, and the list continues. These acts of devastation are NOT a part of God's design for this world. God wants us to live in joy. God wants us to live in peace. God wants us to live in greatness.

Obviously, we are not in God's image in terms of height,

weight, or skin color. God is spirit and uncreated. Still, God made humanity in His own image, which means that there are essential ways in which He has made us to be like Him. We have self-awareness. We can communicate, plan, think, create, design, build, solve problems, and be a force for good in our world. Moreover, we can definitely LOVE!

We were born to be fully human, fully mature, and fully happy. Who you are inside will go with you throughout your life; what you have on the outside, whether possessions or acclaim, will not. Do not be afraid of having enough. Seize every day you have left to add to the former things. Often it takes a long time to discover why you were born. Sometimes it happens very suddenly!

CHAPTER 2
WHO ARE Y.O.U.?

"Get to know who YOU are and do not allow people to mishandle Y.O.U."

Lady Cj

I grew up with two other sisters, Pam and Nett. We were so close in age that people actually thought we were triplets when we were younger. Our mother, Alma, aka "Ma'Dear," made most of our clothes. She was an excellent seamstress as well as a great cook. Whatever clothes we saw in the store, she made it! She would allow us to go to a store called Cloth World and pick out patterns and material. Of course, yours truly always wanted something different or something unique. We did not know what hand-me-downs were because Ma'Dear was always on her sewing machine. Because of closeness in age, body sizes (slim at that time), our neighborhood nicknames were Chocolate, Strawberry and Vanilla. Yes, we were the Neapolitan ice cream! For some reason, my Vanilla eventually became nicknamed "Red."

Dressing up, pretending to be a doctor, nurse, teacher, astronaut or movie star was a normal day of play for my sisters and me. Wearing high heel shoes and putting on make-up and long dresses made us feel special. We felt like movie stars living in Hollywood. Going to church from sunup to sundown was also a normal part of our lives. We participated in BYPU (Baptist Young People's Union), Sunshine Band, usher board, choir, and other citywide church events. Later on, I became one of the Youth Directors in the church, which further ignited my passion for people. However, as involved as I was in these numerous activities and organizations, when I was alone, a lingering question remained. "Who are Y.O.U.?" I pondered on these questions often, *"Who Am I?" "Why Am I Here?" "What Am I Here to Do?"*

The purpose of your life is to discover who you are. You have to learn what you are made of and what you are made for. You have to be willing to give yourself some very special attention. Stop *"going" "doing"* and *"chasing."* Start spending time being yourself. You have to connect with your unconditioned self to find out the original essence of who you are. Your unconditioned self wants you to know Y.O.U. (**Y**our **O**wn **U**nique-ness).

Throughout the years, we meet so many people. There are

people who will try to distract, destroy, and duplicate you. Put them in categories once you identify them. We all have relatives, friends, co-workers, or acquaintances whose behavior often defies logic. They are emotionally draining and, by definition—toxic. The problem with these people is, they are infectious like a disease, and if you are not careful—they utterly and completely try to *destroy* you.

It is a well-known cliché that you become exactly like the people with whom you surround yourself. If you hang with alcoholics in a bar all day and all night, it won't be long before you need to stand up in front of a small group, introduce yourself, and proclaim your addition too. It is human nature, so choose your friends and associates carefully. Stay away from negative, toxic people. Identify them quickly and leave them alone. Toxic people will wait on you to die, and they try harder each day to kill Y.O.U. (**Y**our **O**wn **U**nique-ness).

The best way to discover your purpose is to live a purpose-centered life. This simply means to focus on and be receptive to the highest purpose of every situation in which you find yourself. For example, before you attend a meeting, you might say a prayer, *"Dear God, show me the purpose of me being here."* Before an important conversation with a friend, you might want to connect with your heart and think about what the real purpose of your friendship is. Before you even get out of bed in the morning, you might want to choose how you want to feel today. I look in my mirror and roar like a tiger. I occasionally say, *"Good morning. I claim NO lack. Today is going to be the greatest day of my life!"* or *"Good morning. I am going to have an awesome and amazing day!"* Trust me. You will encounter obstacles; you will have oppositions, but if you cannot control the situation, do not worry about it. Keep it moving and let everyone hear you roar!

CHAPTER 3
ACCEPT... Y.O.U.

"Do not allow negative people to drain you; focus on things that matter!"

Lady Cj

For many people, self-acceptance is hard to come by on any good day. On a bad day, when you have made a mistake or two, do not like how you look or feel miserable, your self-acceptance puts you in a bad wreck with Y.O.U. Sometimes I have to look in the mirror and say, *"you better check yourself before you wreck yourself!"* It does not matter how we feel. We are not in control of everything. We have to accept life, circumstances, and mishaps and keep it moving! God is fully in control.

Do not allow people to box you in. Negative people create negative things. Positive people can help shape you into Y.O.U. Focus your energy on what you can control. You can only control Y.O.U. Do you know what is most authentic about you? What do you want people to know about you? Who are you without your ego?

In order to accept who you are, you have to self-accept yourself. Early in life, we begin to construct a persona to help cope with the demands of being in a family, going to school, and eventually facing the world. When you do a close self-inspection, you find that your persona or ego is made of judgments about who you are, what is possible, what you deserve, and what you do not deserve. These judgments become the lens through which you see yourself and the how the world sees you.

You probably know someone who has created a persona commonly described as a perfectionistic. Individuals with this personality type focus on getting things right and being good. Perfectionists have a conceived ideal of self (rather than a real self... Y.O.U.). They have unusually high standards, high expectations, and strict rules they must try to live. Their persona causes them to judge their efforts and makes them feel helpless. The more you judge yourself, the more you move out of alignment with the distinguished goodness of your undefined self.

The more you judge yourself, the less you can see who you

really are. Habits of self-judgement cause you to belittle yourself, criticize yourself, punish yourself, and treat yourself without kindness. The most powerful way to undo these efforts is through kindness and forgiveness. Continuing to self-judge yourself is like beating your head against a brick wall. You already know that your head is soft and the bricks are hard. At the end, you are bruised and broken from self-affliction, things that you caused to happen to you. Treat yourself with kindness.

At any given moment in your life, you are either accepting yourself or rejecting yourself. It is ego versus essence. Rejection means you often say no to yourself: no to your real desires, no to having any needs, no to stopping and relaxing, no to making time for yourself, no to letting yourself be helpful and no to loving yourself more. The real Y.O.U.

When you continue to reject yourself, you live in constant fear of rejections by others. We fashion a persona that tries to be good, tries not to ask for anything, tries not to be a burden, and tries to please people wherever and whenever possible. Little do we realize that living with a fear of rejection will make us feel unlovable, no matter how hard we try to love others! The self-rejection causes us to be mean to ourselves, thus we have no attention, no care, no appreciation and no self-love. Accepting yourself is love. Your capacity to love yourself determines your capacity to love everyone else. The less you accept yourself, the more your friends will criticize you. You must see yourself through the eyes of love. If you are like most people, you know exactly what you do not love about yourself, but you are likely ambiguous and uncertain about the ways that you do love yourself. For example, you could easily write a list of things you do not like about your body, your hair color, the cellulite on your thighs (LOL), the size of your feet, or the number on the scale, but how easily could you write a list of the ways you do love yourself? When you see yourself through the eyes of love, everyone in your life will benefit. If your dad made millions of dollars, but neglected his family, how would that make you feel? If your mother had taken better care of herself, would your childhood have been any better? If your siblings fought all the time and never came around, would you say you didn't have a family? While you cannot go back into your past, you can begin to nurture yourself now. Love Y.O.U. It is essential to understand the difference between self-acceptance and self-improvement if you are to discover your real value. Self-acceptance starts with the awareness that you are whole, innately good; lovable just as you are; and endowed with God-given talents and qualities to share with the world.

Self-improvement, on the other hand, usually starts with the belief that something is lacking in you. Your ego will set in and make you think that you deserve admiration and applause. The problem with self-improvement is that you are trying to improve upon a self that you have not really gotten to know yet. Self-improvement causes you to overlook your true nature and being. No amount of self-improvements, such face-lifts, boob smaller or larger, weight loss, etc. can make up for any lack of self-acceptance. The essence of who you are is already inspiration-packed, wisdom-infused, and blessed with talents and gifts. Building a successful image of yourself is not necessary. Y.O.U. are already good enough. So often, self-improvement is full of musts, thoughts and should or should haves. We have to shift from blaming and doubting. We must accept, allow, trust, and be tolerant. Unfortunate things happen, but you can still have a life of peace.

When you have peace of mind, you cannot only accept who you are; you can learn how to celebrate who you are. One of the biggest days of my life is celebrating my birthday each year. Some of my birthday celebrations are purposed-driven, some are fun-driven, and some are just to do whatever I want to do. You can find more fulfillment when Y.O.U. celebrate others. One year during my birthday celebration, I celebrated and honored my mother and two of my dear friends (the late Merlynn Gill and the late Carrie Stagg). Both of these friends are resting in the Master's arms. In celebration of them, I chose to host a comedy show along with my special guest and friend, the one and only, Comedian Marcus D. Wiley. It was a sold-out event with over 300 people. We got the opportunity to tell them that we loved them, as well as to show them. Proceeds were given to Surviving Angels in their honor.

Always make it a point to congratulate and celebrate others. Stand on the principle of rejoicing with those who rejoice and sow seeds of blessing. It will always open the door for victory in your own life in return!

"God sees Y.O.U. as one of His greatest masterpieces!"

Lady Cj

CHAPTER 4
DO WHAT Y.O.U. DO!

"Never be comfortable in being someone else. Always look within yourself and be confident in who you are and doing what you love to do. Hopefully, it's doing Y.O.U."

Lady Cj

Some say if you work all day and all night, you are a workaholic. I discovered, throughout my years of working, I made my jobs my passion and my purpose. I worked hard, but only to make a difference.

Purpose without meaning is not a purpose. It is simply a filler. When you know what you value, the things that mean most to you in yourself, in others, and out there in the world, then you are able to anchor any activity or behavior to a sense of something that genuinely matters, always bringing your work alive with purpose.

For example, if you value making contributions, you will find purpose by looking for ways you can contribute to a group or give back to a community. If you value laughter, you will be ready with a smile in your business relationships and always be generous with your humor. If you value your connections, openly connecting with and sharing with the people around you will give you purpose.

I have been working since the age of 13, so working absolutely became a lifestyle. During the summer months of my youth, my siblings and I would clean up and work in the church office at the Mt. Sinai Baptist Church, our foundational church. We mopped the floors, polished the instruments, and sang and played in the sanctuary at least twice a week. I loved typing on the typewriter in the office so much that I started helping with the church bulletins, not knowing then that working in a church office would become my way of life. I eventually started working at the Recreation Center at Mt. Sinai Baptist Church. This experience helped to nurture my work ethic. YES, I must go on record thanking Dr. Samuel J. Gilbert, Sr., Pastor Emeritus of the Mt. Sinai Baptist Church, not only for my spiritual foundation but also for affording me my very first job. He made sure I was rooted in the Word and was grounded in good soil for several years.

Later, I worked at Popeye's Fried Chicken at the age of 15 as a part-time cashier. Most of my co-workers were my classmates from Regan Senior High School. Sam Gilbert, II, son of Dr. Samuel Gilbert, Sr., hooked me up with this job. Our Popeye's Manager was easygoing and spent time teaching us the ropes of how to excel in employment. After six months of training, I became a part-time manager. My position as manager provided great opportunities. I made much more money and was able to hire other employees and give back to our community.

By the time I reached the 12th Grade, I had worked at Shell Oil Company through Reagan Senior High School's Vocational Occupational Educational (VOE) Program as a File Clerk. I was the youngest person in our department. During my senior high school, I was also preparing to attend college. I received acceptance letters to Texas Southern University, Blinn Jr. College, Sam Houston State University, and Prairie View A&M University. I could not wait to leave home and go to college, so I thought. In reality, I started weighing my options. I had that mind over money feeling.

One month before graduating from high school, a new manager for Shell Oil Company employed out of California, needed a secretary. Not having any experience in this field, (but I took typing in the 11th Grade), Mr. Richard Perelman, the Supervisor, hired me as a full-time employee of Shell Oil Company with benefits and taught me the ropes. After a couple of months, I left my part-time job at Popeye's Fried Chicken on 11th Street. He walked me through resigning with integrity. Not only was he my boss, but we also became friends.

Mr. Richard Perelman told me about Shell's educational reimbursement program, so I pursued my education, attended Houston Community College, and took evening classes. Mr. Perelman purchased my first semester books. Maintaining my grades and grade point, which was required through the reimbursement program, I never had to pay for any books throughout my college years because of his first investment. I transferred from Houston Community College to the University of Houston and graduated with a degree in Business Administration.

I was a full-time employee and part-time college student with benefits working in the profit-sharing division of Shell Oil Company. I started typing on a manual typewriter, no computers at that time. Once Shell purchased computers, I was able to enhance our processes and procedures. I created various forms that our managers could use to correspond with our Shell employees who invested in the profit-sharing division. I became a stockholder while I really did not understand the value of stocks. There is a connection to this comment as a stockholder, please continue to read.

After 14 years of employment at Shell, my former boss transferred to another department, and I later applied for another position in the Chemical Division, working in the Meetings and Events Department as an Events Coordinator. Shell Chemical

Company planned up to 40-60 meetings and events a year. In that department, I also helped coordinate one of the largest golf tournaments in the nation, the Shell Golf Classic. I coordinated many seminars, events, and meetings for this organization. I traveled locally and around the county, meeting many people and making connections throughout the oil and gas industry.

After 18 years of employment at Shell, severance packets were offered to employees. I did not fully understand this process; however, as a young and thriving individual, I decided I could move around and do something new and fresh. Besides, my severance packet included a large sum of money and stock that I had invested in and had no clue of its worth. Consequently, I was able to stay off from work for approximately two years. I am still in touch with the many valuable friends I have made over these years. Our savings account increased tremendously.

Shortly after two-year hiatus, it was time for me to hit the job industry again. I began working for the Westin Hotel and Resorts as a Convention Services Manager. Event planning became a way of life. Planning, implementing, and executing are what I grew to love. I handled numerous large accounts servicing the needs of clients such as the Offshore Technology Conference (OTC), National Baptist Convention of America, Annual Oncology Nursing Conference, as well as accounts in the sports and entertainment arena. Once again, I was afforded the opportunity to meet many people, and I made some powerful connections. My name and reputation buzzed throughout the hospitality industry.

I also had an opportunity to meet San Antonio Spurs basketball player David Roberts who had a bad experience at our hotel with his room. I was able to smooth things over and resolve the issue. Out of appreciation, he gave me his basketball jersey. Needless to say, I sold the jersey to one of his fans at the hotel for $800 because this girl does not play those types of jokes. I am a loyal Houston Rockets fan!

Furthermore, while working at the Westin Hotel, I met Magic Johnson and his wife, Cookie, during the Los Angeles Lakers playoff games against the Houston Rockets. Arsenio Hall was also staying in our hotel (that was a joke all by itself). As I was planning a wedding for Rap-o-lot Prince James and his fiancé, I ran into the one and only Magic Johnson. His wife, Cookie, was looking for a place for the cheerleaders to practice in the hotel. I had to really make magic happen, so I ran up to the General Manager's office and requested the Exhibit Hall for their practice. Permission was easily granted. Once they all were settled, I went down the exhibit hall to make certain everything was going as planned. The Johnson thanked me and asked if there was anything they could do for me. I told Magic Johnson I would love for him to meet my boss and some of my co-workers who really did love the Lakers. He immediately agreed. As we walked around the hotel, people were just glaring and amazed. I heard a couple of our employees say, "only Crystal!" She gets to meet every important person who comes to this hotel."

As Magic and I finally approached our department, my girlfriend, Yvette East, was coming out of the area. When he opened the door, she dropped all of her files on the floor and started to scream. Everyone came running out of his or her offices. I said, "Allow me to introduce you all to my friend, Mr. Magic Johnson." He followed my lead and said, "I have known Crystal for years. She is such a jewel." One of my co-workers said, "Yea, right. When is her birthdate?" He said, "November 26." Then he again said, "Yea, right. How many children do she have?" Magic Johnson said, "Two!" We laughed so hard, he stopped all of that foolishness. Little did he know, I had schooled him on our way to the office (LOL). Of course, that gave them a lot to talk about for a long time.

As Magic and I traveled back down to the Exhibit Hall area, eyes and mouths still on us. I laughed and shined at the same time. Cookie, once again, thanked me for the hook-up. The cheerleaders were doing their thing. As I was finally saying my goodbye, Mr. Arsenio Hall walked up. I said (under my breath), "I'm so mad at this man right here." Magic asked me what had happened. I said, "He was very rude and disrespectful to me upon his check-in." Mr. Hall said, "No, I wasn't, what did I do." I stated very nicely (yea, right), he said that his staff sent all of his requirements and everything was not placed in his hotel room." I asked what was missing and he gave me the items. I pulled out the Banquet Event Order

(BEO) and showed him everything that was placed in his room and signed off by our Banquet Captain. Mr. Hall stated that none of those things was in his room. I asked him what his room number was. When he told me, I showed him on the form that this is the room all of those items were placed. Another one of his security team members walked up as we were closing and overheard the ending of the conversation and stated that they moved Mr. Hall to another room because bench of security with one of their team members. Mr. Hall thoroughly apologized, thanked us for our awesome and excellent service. I was selected as Employee of the Year. It gave me fulfillment to another level.

Magic and Cookie Johnson had my personal cellular number and when he opened up Magic Theatres on I-45 North and Crosstimbers, I received a personal invite as their guest. It was simply amazing. Relationships (people) are always key to your passion and purpose.

Another experience at the Westin Hotel and Resorts that is embedded into my mind while servicing a conference called IEEE Advancing Technology for Humanity, (well over 3,000 attendees), there was a clinch in the registration process, long lines and frustrated people. Computers were down and the software did not work. I immediately took control of the challenge, handed all the attendees an index card to complete their registration and once the system came up we would have their badge printed and ready for them to pick up. The technician arrived on site and connected the network. We had badges printed within an hour. After the first session, attendees were able to pick up their registration badges. I encouraged each team to smile and thank the attendees for their patience.

The Vice President of the Greater Houston Convention and Visitors Bureau (GHCVB) received word of how I handled this stressful task and invited me to meet her. After going to lunch with her, we discussed my future; she offered me a job working for the GHCVB organization as the Projects Manager. People will see what is already placed in you to help you to be the best Y.O.U. can be!!!

I started working for the GHCVB within a month after working the IEEE Advancing Technology for Humanity Conference. I became the Special Projects Manager for the City of Houston. I handled over 60 projects a year. I was a part of a powerful team whose primary purpose was to sell the City of Houston to meeting planners all across the country. In addition, during my tenure at the GHCVB, my team was responsible for bidding on bringing the Super Bowl LI to Houston for 2017 at NRG Stadium. Clearly, we were successful at this feat! Let it go down on paper, we did that! There are countless other stories that I could include in this book, but I want to touch on the experiences that helped me make the difference in every job I worked.

Another project my team established was hosting a GHCVB Golf Tournament. NO, I did not play golf. NO, that small white ball did not do anything for me, even though sometimes, when I would go to the practice range, I found myself hitting it out of frustration (LOL). I did get a nice pair of golf clubs and several shoes that I sold to several of my golf friends and gave the money to charity. In planning the tournament, I took the approach that I have applied throughout my life. I reached out to familiar contacts. I was able to secure some of my past relationships to participate and support this annual golf tournament. The financial goal from the tournament was successfully met, and after expenditures were paid, GHCVB rewarded me with an outstanding bonus check. Once again, I had found a way to build my wealth for the future. I also meet many people from all across the country. Some of the individuals with whom I forged relationships were unimaginable and unexplainable. I was in the room with CEO's, CFO's, Presidents, Executives, Managers, Celebrities, and Athletes most of whom became my good friends. Some of them pulled me, and some of them pushed me, but I knew my value and my worth. I tried to bring much to the table. Key relationships remained the focus.

I worked hard, I played hard, and I prayed hard. My reputation as a hard worker followed me; some would say I am a workaholic. I did not have to spend much time proving myself. Knowing I was hired to make a difference wherever my feet landed has always been my strive and thrive.

After a couple of years at GHCVB, we got a new president, and boy was he hard to work with, for he devalued everyone. He did not seem to care about anyone but himself. He nearly drove all of the sales managers crazy, so much so that many of them resigned, quit, or retired early. I struggled under his leadership because he was a piece of work, but I remained focused and worked hard as the Project and Events Manager. We continued to bring conventions, conferences, seminars, and large meetings to our city. My income did not change nor did my relationships.

I continued working hard, loving what I was doing, and I kept trying to make a difference. Twice, they offered me a job as a Sales Manager for GHCBV, but I denied the offers. Traveling, attending tradeshows, promoting the City of Houston and truly enjoying what I was doing; for over 5 years.

I always felt like a target. Jealousy and envy always follow a person when you are trying to make it to the top. Someone is always trying to take you down. I was always a no tolerate person. I love to laugh and smile, but work jokes; I never contributed to any of the foolishness. One day, one of the sales managers from one of our hospitality hotels sent me a joke through an email. It was one of the worst jokes I have ever seen regarding African Americans. I did not find it funny at all. I never played the race card, and I really did not know how to respond. I also never played the mommy or daddy jokes. I truly found the joke to be racist, offensive, disrespectful, and disturbing, and I found myself angry. I immediately requested a meeting with our GHCBV President and the person who sent the email. While at the meeting with the president and the person who sent the email, our President said directly to me, "You need to get over the joke and move around." Then, they laughed. I think I turned three shades of red, and I found myself angry for real. I stood up in his office and I told him I quit. I could not be a part of this organization as long as he was the president and there were no consequences for that inappropriate joke sent around this organization. As I was walking down the hallway, the president yelled and said to me, *"You can't quit. You are fired."* At that point, it really did not matter to me. I was totally done. I turned around and said, *"Your loss is my gain."*

As I walked to my assistant's area, I knew I was leaving this organization. I instructed her to send all my personal belongings to my home. I grabbed my purse and left the building. I did not have a worry in the world. I was mad, for real. As the word was buzzing around the hospitality industry that I quit working at the GHCVB, I received numerous calls from hotel directors with offers for me to work for their organization. I decided to lay low.

Now to write at full speed, I stayed at home for several months. I started to watch *"The Young and Restless," "All My Children,"* and *"General Hospital."* I thought I was a soap opera junkie and a couch potato. One day while I was minding my own business and enjoying doing me, I received a phone call from a friend asking if I could come and assist him with the *"Get Out to Vote Campaign"* for November. Of course, I agreed to offer my assistance.

As I was working the campaign wholeheartedly, Lee P.

Brown became the Mayor of the City of Houston. He personally requested a meeting with me and offered me my job back at the GHCVB. I had been enjoying my needed break. It was a time to reflect, refresh, and renew not only my mind but also my body and soul. Our parents always taught us, *"If you don't stand for something, you will fall for anything."* This was my test and I think I passed it well. I did not return to the GHCVB. Three years after leaving this organization, I received commission and investments checks that were due to me. I maintained relationships with so many people I had met while working there, and they reminded me of the difference I made at the GHCVB.

For over 20 years, I went to work without a fulfilling purpose. I had a reason for working, which was to make plenty of money. I wanted to be rich. I wanted to have the finest of things, but working, for this reason, was not the same thing as having a purpose. I had worked since I was 13 years of age. I had gotten promotions after promotions and pay raises, large and small, but many days, I still felt unfulfilled. There is a world of difference between having a job and having a purpose.

"YOU are way too gifted, to work just for a check, always work towards fulfillment!"

Lady Cj

Being busy accomplishing daily tasks was also a normal way of life for me. By nature, I am a producer of tangible products. I work to produce outcomes. The purpose of life, however, is not to be as busy as possible but to be productive as possible. One of the biggest blocks to discovering your purpose is chronic busyness. Being busy in some ways can be purposeful as well as productive, but when you are permanently busy, it is a sign that your busyness conceals a lack of clarity. Your busyness should produce an outcome that touches lives and makes a difference in society.

My life was back on the market again; sadly, it was within months. December 1999, I received a call from this local pastor, who is by the way now, Dr. James Wallace Edwin Dixon, II, senior pastor of The Community Of Faith Church. Pastor Dixon was requesting my administrative services. His Executive Administrator, Church Secretary and Receptionist were out ill, and he was preparing to travel to Israel with a host of his congregants. He needed his sermons typed and their telephones covered in the office. They were traveling to Israel in three days. The phones rang all day long. People had so many answers to their own questions—you will catch that later. Little did I know, the pastor would be dictating his sermons to me while I was also answering the telephones! Why did I ever show him that I was a multi-tasker! This is how they hooked me, and now twenty years later, I am still here. I readily acknowledge it is only by the grace of God that I am still here. Working and serving in this capacity is my passion and purpose. Of course, the intricacies of this job alone are a book waiting to be written and published.

When talking to people, they admit they are not in their purpose. Doing what we really love is necessary if we want to be fully happy. This is why there is so much unhappiness going on in the world; people just are not doing what they are here on earth to do. Finding true passion is not as simple as it may seem. For some, yes, it does come naturally, but most of the time, you have to ask yourself some questions to pinpoint exactly what you were born to do.

What do I have to offer is a question that should always come to mind. When you take someone to the grocery store, you are just a driver. When I took my dad to the barbershop to get his haircut, I was just the driver. Since our kids had graduated from college and left home, I purchased school clothes for several underprivileged kids. I find fulfillment in offering my resources to help someone in need. I also purchase groceries, blankets and socks for several needy and homeless people during the holidays. This gives me so much joy in making someone else's days brighter. Remember, we are created to bless others.

Taking our kids to tee ball, baseball, football, and basketball games was a great experience when they were little, but having two kids with a heavy sports life became hectic and sometimes unbearable. Attempting to get one kid to a game at a certain time while the other one needed to be across town 10-20 minutes later sometimes was truly unmanageable.

Driving here and there, trying to help them achieve their academic and sports-life commitments, sometimes made me seem like I was very passionate and excited about how my life was going. To be honest, it was not passion at all. It simply became *"a parent's duty to help their kids achieve their goals in life."*

Can you think about the things that put a smile on your face? Is there a particular event, a particular topic that makes your whole face just light up? Whatever it is that makes you smile and makes you happy whenever you encounter it, this is a sign of something you are passionate and love. I believe that happiness and passion walk hand in hand. Both certainly require each other. Follow what makes you truly happy. It is a wonderful way to figure out how to do Y.O.U. Think about something that you do or that perhaps you used to do that brings total peace to you when you do it. Peace is happiness, happiness is passion, and your happiness should be doing Y.O.U. (*Y*our *O*wn *U*nique-ness).

CHAPTER 5
VALUE Y.O.U.

"No one can make you feel worthless when you know your worth! You should always be high commodity."

Lady Cj

My father would always say to me, "You are priceless! Always position yourself to be worth more than what you can imagine!" These words helped me to see myself in a different position, so when people would say, "You cannot," I say, "YES, I can!" I love proving society wrong.

Have you ever felt victimized by family, friends, and even bosses? Have you ever felt like people treated you poorly and unfairly at times? It is so easy and definitely a common tendency to blame others, act like you are the innocent one, while seeking out people who will reaffirm the pain that you are feeling and wanting that encouragement, by stating "woe is me." That statement alone will zap you mentally and physically and send you right into a depression zone. When you start to look at things differently and analyze it them a bit, there is one common denominator in each scenario and situation. That common denominator is YOU!

People can only say or do things to you that YOU allow them to say or do! Do not allow people to treat you the way they want to. You bring a lot to the table. Your energy, confidence, and attitude are the currency that should attract others. Do not settle for less. Always believe YOU deserve more. Never settle for being overlooked, or walked on. This is very disrespectful.

You have to create your own destiny with your career, family, friendships, and community. With your career, if you are disliked, so what? If you are mistreated, change your loyalty, dedication, and destination. Again, always believe you can do better, be in a better place, and live a better life. With your friends, embrace the fact that they are all unique pieces of a pie. Some will be lifetime friends that are truly close to the family, some are social friends, and many are simply acquaintances. Know the value of your true friends and know what they bring to your table. It will teach you how to excerpt your energy and who to invest in your life. Do not spend time, money, or energy in negative relationships. Do not allow people to bring you down to their level. Always have a high level that is sometimes unreachable and yes, you can be untouchable at the right time and place.

Throughout our kids' lives, we have taught them not to personally consider everyone their friend. When they were in elementary, middle, high school and college, we taught them that most of their classmates they would meet would likely only remain as associates. You will know when you have true and real friends because you will someday not only call them your friend, but they will become your sisters or brothers *from another mother.* Make sure your inner circle is sacred and thoughtfully selective.

Learn not to tolerate people who do not appreciate you, do not value your heart, who take and take, and who do not call you until they need something. When you tolerate and allow people to disrespect you, it diminishes your self-esteem and your sense of self-worth. You are valuable. Know your worth!

The most important relationship is one with yourself. Embrace self-love. It is healthy and it is real. When you can love yourself the way you are, yes with flaws, because NO ONE is perfect, you will stop apologizing for who you are. We will always be under construction, but right now, learn that you are "perfect" the way you are, right now, right here! You have to learn to love yourself; love will come through you first!

You have to be the gatekeeper of your own self. Your heart is a very precious gift. Your body is the temple. Be very selective. Respect it and be respected at all times. Love yourself and be loved. If you do not respect and love yourself FIRST, building a healthy relationship with anyone is like building a house with NO foundation. You will surely crumble.

Again, know your value and do not accept people treating you less than you deserve. Do not have unrealistic expectations and demands or a sense of entitlement. However, you always deserve for people to treat you the way you treat them and vice versa. The minute you negotiate your self-worth and accept less, you say to this society that you do not deserve better.

You can only be your true self if you know your true value. Knowing your true value gives you the confidence to face life's challenges. It gives the confidence to face rejection. It gives you the confidence to take risks, make mistakes, and get back up again.

"Look at people as a great mirror reflection that can help you to grow, but don't allow them to break or shatter Y.O.U.!"

Lady Cj

CHAPTER 6
ENJOY Y.O.U.

"We do not choose how we are going to die, but we can choose how we are going to live! Enjoy you!"

Lady Cj

I can recall a season in my life when I desperately wanted to change the way I sounded and the way people heard my voice. Growing up in middle and high school, I was a very active and very loud cheerleader. I would practice cheers all day long, even in my sleep. I found so much joy in making up new cheers and chants. Even when I would talk to people, my laugh was very distinguished. I would always hear people say, *"I can hear her; here comes Crystal!"*

People talked about how loud I was and how I always liked to joke and have fun. Sometimes people felt like I was in overkill, but this was my daily lifestyle. At times, I wanted to be quiet, silence my voice, and especially dress down, but that was not me. I love myself, I love the style and I definitely love to dress. Generationally it was passed down through our father by his father. Every time he stepped out, he did not have to "get ready, he stayed ready!" That is what he taught us. This nugget will always be with me for the rest of my life. Of course, when I made changes, people would call me sassy, classy, and stuck-up. I felt as though I was "dammed if I did and dammed if I didn't!" People will try to make you become someone you are not. Temporary changes do not work. If I have said it once, I need to say it again, just simply be YOU!

Society directs us to find enjoyment through pleasing others, working our way up a career ladder, or seeking pleasure through financial, physical, or emotional pursuits. Society's messages are not for our personal success, but make sure you play the game with your own ball. If you are dabbling in life, make sure you always control the ball.

Learning the true meaning of enjoyment was a revelation for me. Our parents encouraged us to pursue enjoyment through what worked for them while hoping to shield us from the sufferings they went through to get to where they are. In order to enjoy yourself, you have to first fall in love with yourself. We usually think of falling in love as a process specific to dating, but in reality, we fall in love in so many different ways and with so many different things. We fall in love with people, places, literature, art, clothes, and even states of mind. There is no wrong way to love. Love begins with Y.O.U.!

Many people, especially women, dream about falling in love at a young age. There is certainly nothing wrong with falling in love, but make sure you love YOU. You are not being selfish because you want to spend some time developing yourself. It is important that we are never so wrapped up in loving others that we forget to love ourselves first! Spend time with Y.O.U.R-SELF. Learn to appreciate yourself the same way you would appreciate the one you love.

Examine the things in life that you love to do. For example, you may enjoy taking someone to the grocery store or to the doctor, or you may simply enjoy spending breakfast, lunch, or dinnertime with your loved ones. Do not forget about the family reunions, family and friends days, family picnics, and family vacations you love to attend. Enjoying all these things with others is great, however, you cannot be the best you, if you do not love and take time to care for Y.O.U.

Not only loving and taking care of you, but you must also embrace Y.O.U. Learning your quirks-because your quirkiness is what makes you Y.O.U. See your beauty in your birthmarks. Enjoy time spending with your own thoughts, rather than shying away from them. Loving yourself ranges from learning about you, learning about your needs, and especially learning how to meet your needs. You must acknowledge your value and self-worth. Embrace everything about yourself, including the good and the bad. None of you is bad; there are things we will need to improve, enhance or embrace.

You should only be the one thing God created you to be... Y.O.U. Do your thing! #doyou! So many people twist themselves up in knots trying desperately to be something or someone else. Do not become exhausted trying to fulfill some endless list of qualities and capabilities that you think will make you feel loved, safe, or happy. That is not the way to live. I know because I have done it. Many of us, if we are honest, we have wandered far from what we were created to be. Never get wrapped up in what someone else wants you to be. You do not need anybody's approval to be Y.O.U.!

If you are not enjoying Y.O.U., go back to your essentials, and rediscover the love, skills and passions God planted right inside of you. Look at the threads of your passions that you are carrying throughout your life. If it brings you great joy and fulfillment, you are definitely on the right track!

Think about your adolescent self, your child self, the "you" you have always been. You are a sacred, beautiful collection of passions and capabilities right onto your heart: What do you love? What bubbles your passion?

For most of my adult life, I have been peeling off the layers of expectations, pressure and protecting those precious things in my life that I love. Culture will try to define what it means to be a woman or a man, what it means to be successful, and what it means to live a valuable life. Embracing those, definitions require us to live on a treadmill—really, both literally and figuratively. You will always hustle to fit in to be thin, young and sparkly, sparkly enough, to have extremely large and spotless homes, to have children who are well mannered and clean-faced, and...our dreams orderly and profitable. It is not really life, that is just living a blessed life. You need to have total fulfillment by doing you, to have a life full of joy and meaning.

You are rare, one of a kind, valuable, and precious. You have to become successful in being yourself. In order to do this, you have to speak good things to yourself daily. *"When I was born, I was created to be successful, remarkable, and powerful!"* That is my personal affirmation.

Never compare yourself with others. When God created us, he created a variety. We look differently, and we definitely come in all shapes and sizes, whether small, large, tiny, or huge. We are distinctive right down to our fingertips. There will never be two of you!

Focus on your potential instead of your limitations. Refuse to concentrate on your weaknesses in an effort to turn them into strengths. Keep your flaws in perspective. People with high levels of confidence have just as many weaknesses as those without confidence, but they focus on their strengths instead of their weaknesses. Stay focus on you!

Walk away from roles and expectations that other people have for you. Live in peace with the exact way Y.O.U. were created – on purpose and for a purpose. Discover what or whom you need to leave behind, in order to recover that essential self that you were created to be. Whatever you need to walk away from in order to reclaim those unique parts that you were designed to be, be willing to do so. Do Y.O.U. (**Y**our **O**wn **U**nique-ness)!

Criticism is real and a very hard thing to face and deal with. Society shows us much criticism. The workplace shows us so much criticism. Even the church shows us criticism. Some things you do or say will make people criticize you and critic you. They say you cannot wear this to work; your hair cannot look like this; your shoes are inappropriate for work, and on and on. When you dare to be different, you will have to expect some criticism. Going along with the crowd when you know that in your heart that is not the right way is one of the reasons people do not succeed at being themselves. It is important to always be you!

Even if you find yourself standing alone, you have to move forward and do not compare yourself with others. Do not try to be someone you are not. One of the greatest challenges in life is being yourself in a world that is trying to make you be like everyone else. Someone will always be thinner, someone will always be prettier, someone will always be younger, someone will always be smarter, but they will never be YOU! Do not change so people will like you. Be yourself and the right people will love the real YOU. Be proud of who you were made to be. You are the best person you can be!

CHAPTER 7
Y.O.U. MUST BE THE PRIORITY

"Make yourself a priority. It is not selfish or self-centered. It's necessary!"

Lady Cj

If you do not take care of yourself, the question is, *"Who will?"* Some people view the words *"Me"* and *"YOU"* as being selfish and self-centered. While this negative perception may be valid in some situations, it is not true in all cases. You must spend some time focusing on yourself because you can NEVER be any good to anyone else without knowing how to first love and treat yourself.

Most people think that "business" is the number one top priority, and family life comes in second. The logic behind this thinking is we need to make money in order to care for our family. That is perfectly understandable because, on some level, it feels right. After all, you have to put a roof over your family's head and food on the table, so when the laundry is not finished but the bills are paid, we feel rightly justified in our decision. However, that is fine if it is working out for you. You will discover that if it is not really working out for you, and despite all that you do, you are still struggling to progress your business, and your home life is miserable and it is tipping you closer to a breaking point–***your top priority needs to be YOU!*** You are the business. Without you, you cannot work, you cannot make money and "if you don't work, you don't eat!" Therefore, without you, there is no real business.

Again, it is vital that you look after number *ONE*. You need to be at your best physically, emotionally, spiritually and mentally, but you will not be anywhere near your best if your relationships are strained, your health is deteriorating, and you are living in an environment of constant chaos and disorder. You can surely get by like that for a while, but it is not a good strategy for long-term success.

People who have meaning and purpose in their lives are happier, feel more in control and get more out of what they do. They also experience less stress, anxiety and depression. It is easy to bog yourself down, especially in the craziness of everyday life, and push your own needs aside. When you do this, not only do you suffer, but also you are not your best for everyone else around you. You will actually be a better human if you put yourself first – so start doing these things.

Priority #1: **Y.O.U.**

- Invest in yourself and stack the odds in your favor.
- Work on your personal development so that you can grow beyond the fears and worries that hold you back.
- Do more of the things that matter and less of the things that do not.
- Invest in fulfilling a dream or higher purpose.
- Do not allow other people to waste your time, and do not dare waste your own time. **RECLAIM YOUR TIME!**
- Learn to say "no" to other people and things.
- Get enough sleep so that you can function with a clear head.
- Do things that constantly reinforce self-belief and prove to your own mind that you are capable.
- Take small steps, look for little victories, and allow those wins to spur you on to do and achieve more.
- Protect your most valuable and productive state of mind, and do not allow it to destroy you.
- Create and maintain a great environment in which to live, love, and laugh.
- Look after your body and your health.

- Exercise a little more and eat a little less. Yes, that means eating healthier.
- Read more books and watch less TV.
- Spend more time with YOU.

Priority #2: Your Family

I want to share my amazing life with the people I love. You can never get back those precious moments that are so priceless. It is so easy to wrap yourself up in work, feeling so desperate to make it work at all costs, that you push your family away. You may hear, *"You care more about your job than your family."* Some will say, *"Is that job really that serious?"* Still, others may say, *"You work, work, and work; you should be a billionaire by now."* For short periods, your family may be able to understand your need to get absorbed in your work, but if they feel you are constantly neglecting them, they will feel distant and excluded.

Here are some elements I used to make *Family Priority #2*:

- It is essential that we breathe and we eat. Family time must be just as essential. Our family should be the most important aspect of our life next to our faith, so it only makes sense to spend quality time with them. It should be a non-negotiable factor. Plug in family time where it makes the most sense: mealtimes, bath times, driving, etc. You do not have to make it hard on yourself because you are doing these things anyway. Make the most of these opportunities by making them moments to enjoy each other's company.

- Every busy family knows that the key to getting to every appointment, practice, and getting food is having a schedule you can stick to on a consistent basis. So, why not schedule and plan family time? It sounds quite simple enough, but it is not really. How do you fit one more thing into your busy schedule? Literally, Y.O.U. just do it. For example, at the start of every school year, we would sit down and plan our calendars. It included daily schedules, time for homework, and our time to eat dinner. In addition, we would plan for designated family time.

- Each family member must have mutual accountability. This probably sounds formal, but it is so necessary. We have to allow our children to hold us accountable for family time. If we do not, family time will be lost. Most importantly, our children will lose faith in how much we value spending time as a family. We need to communicate to our children that spending quality family time is important because our family is most important. The way to communicate that is to allow them to hold us accountable when it seems like other things are getting in the way.

- We have to value our children as individuals; they are separate beings. If you have more than one, love them, be the model and show appreciation for what makes each of them unique. Celebrate each other as a family.

Well, of course, it all starts with Y.O.U. Know that Y.O.U. are an essential element of your family's family time. Y.O.U. need to be there. Y.O.U. need to be engaged. Y.O.U. have to put your phone down. Understand the laundry can wait another 30 minutes. You can clean the kitchen after they have gone to sleep. You can pick up toys tomorrow. You can DVR that favorite show. Facebook with be there after you finish playing Monopoly, Life or Uno. Remember, **Y.O.U.** are modeling behaviors and philosophies for your family.

When our children were growing up, we made our family time on Friday nights. We ordered pizza, watched movies, and even had talent shows. Our son loved music. He had a mic and a drum set. He would sing and beat at the same time. Our daughter loved to dance. Whatever we did on family night, we loved doing it. Later on, as our children became teenagers, our son and I would tell jokes. We were stand-up comedians. We would laugh and laugh for long periods. My hubby did not find too many of our jokes funny, but he would bear it. We help fuel each other and instill in our children, family matters. As a result, we have a bond that cannot be broken.

Because my hubby and I showed that we genuinely

enjoyed spending quality time with our family, there was no doubt in our children's minds and hearts we loved them. They gain confidence and self-assurance, and they love better because they have experienced love. To this day, our children are best friends. They are so close; they live one apartment away from each other. It will not surprise us when they purchase their new homes and live in the same neighborhood. It is very safe to say that we all want to raise confident, successful adults who model God's love for others, give of themselves, and shower them with love.

Make time to be with your family, they will be the ones to share in your triumphs when you have achieved the success you are hoping for and they will be the ones to pick up the pieces if it does not work out.

Priority #3: Your Business

Whatever it is Y.O.U. do that you call working from home, whether it be studying for professional qualifications, blogging, or working remotely as an employee or as an entrepreneur, it is a major priority.

Working as an employee or being your own boss should be important to you, but do not let your work become an obsession to the point where it causes Y.O.U. to neglect yourself or your family.

Priorities change depending on what other factors are at play. There will be times when work becomes your top priority and you put it ahead of your own needs and your family's needs, and that is OK for a short while. Numbering these 1, 2, 3, does not mean that they are actually going to happen in this order. Remember, a person who does not work will not be able to eat!

Sometimes you might feel guilty about putting yourself first, but it is necessary. Just as when you are on an airplane that suffers sudden decompression, you need to put on YOUR own oxygen mask first before YOU assist others, including your own family, or you might not be able to help them at all. It takes just 30 seconds to lose consciousness at 35,000 ft., so put YOUR own mask on first! How you choose to prioritize is up to Y.O.U., but for me, the revelation about putting yourself first comes from my personal experience. I have tried all the other combinations and this one is by far the best. It is ok to do Y.O.U.!

CHAPTER 8
NEW BEGINNINGS
IT IS ALL UP TO Y.O.U.

"Every story has an end, but in life you can start your
new beginning today.
Forget about the past; press toward your future, Do Y.O.U.!"

Lady Cj

All good books have an ending and it is time to close. I am definitely ending this book the way it was started, with Y.O.U. (*Y*our *O*wn *U*nique-ness) in mind.

Let me try to come to a broader conclusion. I choose to close this book with Chapter 8. The number eight has been meaningful in my life throughout this journey. The number 8 is a symbol of balance, which means that this number will help you maintain the balance between your material and spiritual life. When you accept the presence of number 8 in your life, you will receive divine wisdom and you will live in peace and harmony. At this juncture, this is absolutely where I reside, in peace and harmony.

Doing Y.O.U. is basically what anyone needs to do. Find your own unique-ness, capitalize on it, and discover your purpose and passion. It will keep you from complaining about anything. If Y.O.U. is stuck in a dilemma, Y.O.U. are the person who has to fix it. When you lose all regard for other people's opinions and you obtain peace with yourself, Y.O.U. is all that matters. Do know that you will attract haters, jealous, and envious people, when you do Y.O.U.! You cannot do Y.O.U. surrounding yourself with negative people. Survive to make a difference in society and touch other people lives. Be caused driven to make a difference.

Some people look at doing Y.O.U. as selfish, inconsiderate, self-centered, self-seeking, self-serving, wrapped up in yourself, but it is not. When you make yourself feel better about Y.O.U., it helps Y.O.U. to make other people feel better.

In today's society, people need to understand doing something without the fear of judgment is so freeing, but at the same time, they need to think of who they really are and what a positive difference Y.O.U. can make. Stay true to who Y.O.U. are and do it proudly. Express yourself in a way that you are confident without going to the extreme and becoming something or someone who Y.O.U. are not.

Doing things for yourself can be good because everyone needs some time to reflect on life. However, this does not mean that you cannot do things without friends and family. Have the people who love and care for you join you on your adventures because they will make those times better. They will support you since they know the real you and what you love to do. They will love to join you in doing what you love to do because they love you and want to see you happy.

Always do Y.O.U. with love. Love yourself, but then once you get that far, spread that love. Do things you love, as you do this, people will see that you love what you do, whether it is your occupation or hobby. The passion you show will provoke other people to pursue what they want to do. Even though you are doing Y.O.U., you are essentially helping others as well to do themselves. What a journey! I cannot wait to hear the stories that will be subtracted from this book. It has been a long time coming; I have to decide to do me!

Start your New Beginning today by simply
*Doing **Y.O.U.** (**Your Own Unique**-ness)!*

MEET THE AUTHOR

Crystal Jackson (Lady CJ) is well known for saying, *"Making It Do What It Do!"* **#doyou (**Y**our** O**wn** U**nique-ness)!** She has lived victoriously in these past years of life, looking for ways to help others discover and embrace the Y.O.U. **(**Y**our** O**wn** U**nique-ness)** in YOU!

Through her life experiences, she has learned to think about ways to improve how she values God first, her family second and how to treat others to live a healthy, hopeful, and happier life. No matter how people devalued her, she has always been confident in who she really is. She embraced her total Y.O.U.

She has now committed her life to help others to discover who they are, embrace who they are and learn how to love Y.O.U. She is a native Houstonian and loves H-Town whole-heartedly!

In her newest released book, "Do Y.O.U. (*Y*our *O*wn *U*nique-ness)", this new and upcoming author Lady CJ takes us through her personal and transformative journey that ultimately led her to these moments of living her best and most blessed life.

Life is a journey, sometimes it can be a roller coaster. It is up to Y.O.U. to continue the ride and never stop fulfilling your life's dreams and accomplishing your goals, always reach HIGHER and dream BIGGER!

"Do Y.O.U." (*Y*our *O*wn *U*nique-ness), is an easy read. The nuggets and applications are life changing. Join Lady CJ on her mission to help facilitate and transform the lives of people all over the world.

Lady CJ sees you in your future, and you already look better! You too, should do Y.O.U. (*Y*our *O*wn *U*nique-ness)!

Stay in touch!

Facebook.com/Crystal Jackson

Instagram.com/Ladycj4real

Twitter.com/Ladycj4real

www.ingramcontent.com/pod-product-compliance
Lightning Source LLC
Chambersburg PA
CBHW061301140726
47998CB00006B/2316